# Quilts among the Plain People

## by Rachel T. Pellman and Joanne Ranck

a People's Place Booklet

Good Books

# Photograph Credits

Cover photos: Kenneth Pellman

Beth Oberholtzer—5, 7, 17, 19, 31 (top), 34, 37, 38, 40—(detail), 41, 43, 45, 51, 52, 53, 56, 58, 60, 61, 62, 65, 66, 69, 70 (left and bottom), 71, 77, 87, 96. Richard Reinhold—6, 11, 22, 25, 27, 28, 31 (bottom), 35 (top and bottom), 39, 40 (top), 42, 44, 47, 54, 70 (right), 73 (top), 74 (right). Steve Scott—8, 10, 59, 67. Kenneth Pellman—9, 21, 26, 29, 30, 46, 48 and 49, 50, 55, 57, 63, 68, 72, 74 (left), 75. James Strickler—13. Alma Mullet—15. Perry Cragg—33, 90. MCC/Steve Goossen—73. Fred J. Wilson—88. MCC/Jim King—89.

Design and illustrations by Craig Heisey.

QUILTS AMONG THE PLAIN PEOPLE
Copyright © 1981 by Good Books, Lancaster, PA 17602
International Standard Book Number: 0-9346-7203-2
Library of Congress Catalog Card Number: 81-82209

# Contents

# 1. Beauty Among the Austere

Why do many Amish and Mennonites who are devoutly committed to a simple, austere life make beautiful quilts? Who are these people who disdain fashion and convenience, yet cultivate exquisite artistry in color and stitching?

There is no denying the fact that life in the Old Order Amish and Mennonite communities is dramatically disciplined. Both large and small matters in life are governed by what the brotherhood believes. One's dress, mode of transportation, vocation and entertainment are affected by commonly held convictions and strong social pressures within the group. But these boundaries have distinct advantages. There is freedom in knowing limits and inside these limits is great room to grow.

Appreciation for beauty is not lost when life is austere. Rather, it seems intensified. It becomes more vivid in minute details. Flower beds and gardens are tended with love and care. There is delight in the breakthrough of a bean sprout not only because of the food it eventually brings but for the joy of seeing a full straight row of new green shoots. Flower beds bring new delight every year with the marvels of bright colors. Beauty in nature is admired heartily.

Among these people personal beauty is handled more gingerly. There is no room for individual pride within the fellowship. Regulations on dress and lifestyle are in part to squelch temptations toward vanity. But the line here is delicate. In work, a job well done is imperative, yet pride in that job is not tolerated. Doing it well is only doing what is expected. But there are exceptions, and quilting may be one of them. Here is an avenue where a woman may show off her abilities unashamedly. In a community where restraint inhibits public displays of emotion and physical contact, a quilt shows love much the same way a favorite food is carefully prepared as a display of affection.

*Appreciation for beauty is not lost when life is austere. Rather, it seems intensified. It becomes more vivid in minute details such as flowers, gardens, and quilts.*

6

*Quilt patterns are a reflection of daily living and working. They are also mirrors of nature. Note the light to dark contrast on the top photo. Field designs (bottom) repeat the straight lines of the Log Cabin quilt (above).*

*An Old Order woman is fulfilled and contented as a mother, homemaker and helper to her husband, family and friends. These roles are expected within the community, and, for the most part, enjoyed.*

# A Marriage of Beauty and Usefulness

Quilting is not solely a Mennonite and Amish art. It is done by women and men all over the world. With a growing awareness of the world's limited resources and renewed interest in getting back to basics, quilting has surfaced as an art worth reviving.

Quilting has survived among these frugal simple people because a quilt is not only a piece of art. It is also functional. Even though a quilt may be a "good" one, folded away in the bedroom chest except for Sundays and holidays, the fact remains that it could be used.

A quilt legitimately displays a woman's ability as a seamstress, quilter, and color co-ordinator. She may show her quilts for the admiration of relatives or friends without intimidation. These reflect on her personally as does a well-kept home, lawn and garden.

Quilting has been termed a salvage art. Small snippets of new fabric left over from other sewing projects or old pieces

**Rachel Petersheim** is one of a family of eleven children. Her mother made three quilts for each of them. Even with that background, the quilting bug didn't bite Rachel till she was a mother herself.

However, at age forty, she has made a career of quilting. She got started one day about six years ago when she and her sister decided to try piecing a Dahlia. That particular Dahlia has never been completed but it was just the beginning of many, many others.

Sewing is relaxation for Rachel, but it is also her job. She disciplines herself to try to get a full eight hours of quilt work in each day. She may begin as early as 5:00 a.m. although since her five children (two girls and three boys) are getting older she says she doesn't get up quite as early. Quilting gets sandwiched between housekeeping, gardening, cooking and mothering. At 5:00 p.m. sewing is done for the day and the evening is dedicated to time with the children.

Rachel sells her quilts but she admits that it is hard to part with them. They become a part of her after giving them so much time and effort. For the Petersheims, quiltmaking is a family affair. The girls help mark patches and the quilting design on the finished tops. The boys help by snipping the strips of patches apart at the appropriate places as Rachel sews them together. Rachel's husband is no longer living. Although he wasn't directly involved in the work, Rachel says "he supported it 100%."

*One of Rachel Petersheim's favorite quilts, the Dahlia, hangs on a pulley washline in front of her home.*

*These people take their faith very seriously because of their history of severe persecution. Their deep concern for modesty and simplicity is expressed in all aspects of life. Note the austerity of this Old Order Amish church building in western Pennsylvania.*

salvaged from yet good parts of worn-out clothing can be used in quiltmaking. Scrap quilts are great fun—each patch has its own story. For many Amish and Mennonites, the salvage impulse is strong. To waste anything is considered irresponsible. Nature and its bounty, as well as personal talent and abilities, are viewed as gifts from God. Each person is held accountable for using these gifts wisely.

## Quilting As a Tradition

Quilting techniques are passed from generation to generation. Quilts themselves are often given to grandchildren or children. Such a bequest is more than just a fabric object. It is hours of time and painstaking effort given in love.

Life in community and on a farm is conducive to quilting. Each small child has chores to do. Boys and girls learn responsibility and hard work early. Little girls, following the example of their mother and grandmother, begin to sew. Additional discipline comes through the tedious work of following a pencil line on small patches. Four or five year-old children are taught to sit and sew on Saturday afternoons. One woman recalls her own experience when as a little girl her mother made her follow a pencil line with tiny even stitches. When they weren't perfect she had to rip them out and re-do them. In her frustration she cried but that only blurred her vision and made sewing even harder. That woman is no worse for her lessons. Today she is an able quilter.

## Quilts in the Life Cycle

Farm and rural life is organized around the work flow of the seasons. So is sewing. Many women find time to quilt during long winter evenings when the family is gathered indoors and the snow blows outside. It is a relaxing pastime but also worthwhile. In the spring and summer, gardening and food preservation take priority; quilting projects are laid aside.

As life has its stages, so do quilts. At a very young age children may be taught the basics of sewing quilt patches. As

*Children are anticipated and joyfully received among the plain people. Childhood is a time of freedom but also the beginning of firm discipline, obedience, and respect.*

11

they grow older fewer boys participate; sewing becomes women's work. A girl feels a sense of pride in being allowed to help stitch a quilt in her mother's frame. It identifies her with grown-up women. And to be allowed to quilt rather than help get lunch at a quilting bee is a statement about one's aptitude in quilting.

Young people generally marry in their late teens and early twenties. A woman's responsibilities then include housekeeping, gardening, and often sewing for the family. Although there are usually stores in areas with a sizeable population of plain folk which stock plain clothing for men, women's cape dresses are almost always homemade. Sewing leaves a woman with a whole collection of fabric ends and snippets. Frugally she will store them, accumulating a collection from which a scrap quilt can be made.

When a young woman goes to housekeeping she is expected to have anywhere from two to thirteen quilts completed and ready for use. At marriage it is not unusual for a girl to receive four to six quilts as a gift from her mother. These will be enough for her to begin her home and use until she is established and has daughters of her own who can help quilt.

Children are seen as a gift from God and are treated as such. Frequently a woman will make a crib quilt in joyful anticipation of a child. Children are disciplined at an early age but not with harshness. It is the parents' desire that their children do right, that inspires their strong but loving training.

Women are always worthwhile. Roles are clearly defined and both male and female duties are viewed with dignity. Many a man will quietly boast of his wife's knack with a needle. Some responsibilities are shared. A woman will work the fields if necessary. Little girls as well as little boys learn to plow.

How do these women with large families, houses, and gardens find time to quilt?

Time is a relative thing. In the Old Order society extended families are common. Three generations live and work on the same homestead. That fact eases life a great deal. If grandmother is too feeble to work outdoors she can still lead a rich and full life helping to entertain children or make quilts indoors. Non-physical labor is often done by the elderly folks.

*Children are viewed as a gift from God and are treated as such. The parents' desire that their children do right inspires their strong but loving training.*

It would be misleading to say that all women in Amish and Mennonite communities quilt. For some, quilting is as natural as housecleaning and gardening. For others, it is tedious work and something they simply prefer not doing. Some women in professional fields know little about sewing or do not have time for it.

# A Quilting

Among a people who shy away from TV, radio, movies, and much entertainment experienced by the larger society, visiting is vital. Visiting happens among family and relatives. It includes friends and neighbors who may drop by for the Sunday noon meal and afternoon; it may be an evening with no purpose other than enjoying the company of another family.

A quilting bee is an all-day visit for a group of women who get together to finish a quilt top. Quiltings may be held anytime although they occur more frequently from late fall through early spring.

There is no regular pattern as to how often quiltings are held. A woman will call family and friends together when she has a top ready to be done.

# Is it Work or Pleasure?

A typical quilting in a home usually involves between eight and sixteen women. They arrive in the morning after the school-age children are given a proper breakfast and sent on their way. Preschoolers come along and with a number of friends enjoy the day as much as their mothers. Children may be asked to keep a supply of threaded needles on hand.

Upon arriving the women are ready to begin work. If the quilt to be completed is not already in the frame, those coming first will help to stretch it and put it in. Each woman then takes her place around the frame and quilting begins.

**Alma Mullet** is a left-handed quilter which always puts her at the corner during a quilting bee. The Double Wedding Ring quilt pattern is special to Mrs. Mullet. Both her mother and grandmother enjoyed the challenge of the circular design and Alma continues the tradition. "It's sorta in the family." It's also nice because the pieces are small and one can use a lot of scraps.

Alma began making quilts when she was about fifteen years old. First was a Ninepatch and secondly a Trip Around the World. The second went into her hope chest. At her marriage she received five more quilts—three from her mother and two from her husband's. Those quilts were used on the Mullet's bed as well as the beds of hired men who stayed with them. Her own family of seven daughters and two sons increased the demand for quilts and she made enough for their use. She recalls somewhat regretfully today that all of those quilts are worn out.

At age 65 Mrs. Mullet finds much of her time occupied with quilts. She can be found many hours of the week supervising as well as participating in activities at the Helping Hands Quilt Shop in Berlin, Ohio.

*Quilts surround Alma Mullet, seated left, in this photo with her friends (left to right) Joan Miller, Edna Troyer, and Ruth Weaver.*

*Among a people who shy away from television, radio, movies, and much entertainment experienced by the larger society, visiting is vital.*

It may take a while to be seated. There is good natured jesting about where to sit. No one wants to be next to the fastest quilter because she will be ready to "roll" before they are. Straight lines are easier to quilt than curves so the less experienced quilters will sit at those places if they exist.

A large frame is used, allowing the surface of the quilt to be stretched fully open at the start of a bee. Quilting begins around all four sides. Each woman quilts the area in front of her, reaching as far toward the center as she comfortably can. When she can no longer reach, the quilt is ready to be rolled. The two long wooden poles to which the sides of the quilt have been pinned or basted are released from their clamps and the completed part is gently rolled under bringing the distant section close to the edge. The quilt is pulled taut and quilting begins again from the edge. The women follow light pencil lines which create the decorative quilting pattern, with tiny stitches, each one reaching through to connect all three layers of the quilt.

**Guy Martin** explains his quilt hobby as "a talent that was lying dormant for old age." At 71 years old and a deacon in the Mennonite Church, Guy is delighted with quilts. He started piecing quilts at age sixty-six after retiring from a job in a garment factory. His wife Edythe is a quilter and he began by cutting patches for her. That got monotonous and he figured he could probably sew too. He certainly could! During one year he completed 122 quilt tops. His favorite pattern is probably the Lone Star.

Guy and Edythe work as a team. They each have their own sewing machine and their own desk chair on rollers that accommodates their frequent shifts from the cutting table to sewing machines. Much of their work is donated to Mennonite Central Committee, a relief organization of the Mennonite Church.

Cold weather and rain are conducive to Guy and Edythe's production. They like being in their cozy sewing room when the weather is gruff. They are dedicated to their hard work but not driven by it. How many hours a day does Guy work at sewing? "Well, we start after breakfast but then the mail comes and we have to read that . . ." Guy and Edythe treat each day as another gift from God and enjoy it to the fullest.

*Guy Martin discusses different piecing techniques with his wife Edythe.*

The woman hosting the quilting is in charge of the day, seeing that things run smoothly. She also provides a hearty dinner at noon in exchange for the help with her quilt. The meal is remuneration, and it provides an easy and acceptable "out" for women who either should not (because of their less than standard workmanship) or would rather not quilt. These women are given kitchen duty and enjoy it fully.

Being assigned to the kitchen when you would rather quilt can be humbling. It is sometimes the younger girls whose stitches are not yet tiny or neat enough who get that job. To be invited to quilt in a quilting at a young age is an honor.

Conversation around lunch and the quilt frame is jovial and, to say the least, enlightening. It is the place to catch up on all the latest news, household tips, garden hints, home reme-dies, childrearing information, weather, marriage, births and deaths. Conversations become more intimate as the quilt gets smaller and women come closer together. By early afternoon a top can be completed.

## Who Comes to a Quilting?

A quilting may be planned for "sisters day" when a woman invites all her sisters and sister-in-laws as well as other rela-tives to her home. Or she may choose to have a less intimate affair, asking neighbors and friends in general to her quilting. If the quilt is for a special occasion or is being sold and requires expert workmanship the hostess may invite only a select group of top quilters.

## Quilts as an Extension of Love

Quilting bees are not held only in homes. Church groups may have quiltings for an hour or two at their monthly sewing circle. Some volunteer fire companies also hold quiltings several times a year preparing quilts to sell at their benefit auctions.

*Donating quilts for benefit auctions is an extension of love and service (top). The auction is also an occasion for visiting, eating, and finding bargains. Sometimes quilting is done at the sale site (bottom).*

Quilting becomes community work and Amish and Mennonite women frequently lend their skills in support of these volunteer organizations. (These people traditionally support their local fire company since they depend heavily on its services.) Quilting is also one of the ways Mennonites and Amish contribute to relief efforts. The Mennonite Central Committee (MCC) is a world-wide relief organization sending food, clothing, and personnel all over the world. Each year MCC sponsors auctions in various Mennonite communities throughout North America. One of the main attractions at these sales are the gorgeous quilts. Women work throughout the year making the hundreds of quilts sold for relief. It is a gift of time and self and in its giving, a demonstration of love for all humankind. Quilts are rarely signed and seldom given in individual names. They are given in the name of the church.

# Who Are These People?

The faith and community of the Mennonites and Amish today are shaped by their beginnings 450 years ago in Zurich, Switzerland.

That was the time of the Protestant Reformation led by Luther and Zwingli. But there were more radical believers than those two leaders who became dissatisfied when the major reformers seemed content to work their change within the existing state church structures. These more radical thinkers especially questioned infant baptism and felt that the separation of church and state was imperative.

A small group emerged led by Conrad Grebel, Georg Blaurock, and Felix Manz who held that baptism and church membership must be voluntary and therefore accepted only as an adult. Baptism should occur upon one's confession of faith and voluntary commitment to follow Jesus' example of servanthood. They believed in the priesthood of all believers, with each person having an individual relationship with Jesus Christ that is understood and lived within the support and context of a community of faith.

**Minerva Kauffman** is one of those quilters you might be tempted to avoid sitting next to at a quilting bee. She's friendly enough; it's just that her speed and expertise with a quilting needle have put other quilters to shame!

Minerva's love of quilting and her exacting workmanship were learned from her grandmothers. Both grandmothers were great quilters and she grew up wanting to be just like them. At age thirteen they taught her that she must "do it right or not do it at all." Minerva soon preferred quilting over housekeeping chores. Fortunately her mother's choices were exactly opposite so that when there was a quilt in the frame, Minerva had plenty of opportunity to practice her skills. Her own daughters (she has four boys and three girls) are also avid quilters.

At fifty, Minerva's favorite quilting time is in the early morning. She likes to get up at 5:00 a.m. and quilt for a while before anyone else stirs. In the morning she has time to meditate and enjoy the quietness.

Binding a quilt is Minerva's least favorite aspect. She takes one out of the frame, puts the next one in, and quilts for awhile before she forces herself to do the binding on the completed one. Although she dislikes the job, she does most of it herself because she feels a good binding is imperative on a well-made quilt. She describes herself as being perhaps "abnormally fussy." In the end, what her grandmothers taught her years ago pays off today in gorgeous quilts.

*Minerva Kauffman likes to get up at 5:00 a.m. and begin quilting before anyone else stirs.*

*Nature and its bounty, as well as personal talents and abilities are viewed as gifts from God.*

Outsiders nicknamed the group Anabaptists, meaning rebaptizers. Their numbers grew rapidly. Because of their radical faith they were severely persecuted. Many were killed and many others fled to other parts of Europe and eventually to America. With them went firm commitment and the understanding that they needed the support of each other to follow God fully. They were eventually called Mennonites, a label taken from one of the group's most prominent leaders, Menno Simons.

Ever concerned with right living, several Mennonite leaders became involved in a debate in 1693 concerning discipline in the church. One of them, Jacob Amman, felt that to maintain purity in the church, wayward members should be excommunicated and shunned or ostracized by the rest of the group. There was disagreement among the bishops as to how severe this shunning should be. Amman felt that he must hold to his conviction and so left the group taking some members with him. That fellowship became known as the Amish.

Today there are numerous groups of Mennonites and Amish. Many splits have occurred over the years. Yet basic tenets of faith remain very similar. The differences among the groups are in various understandings of how life-style reflects discipleship to Jesus Christ.


# Origins of Quilting

Amish and Mennonites may take no credit for beginning quilting! Instead, it is an ancient art, likely appearing before the time of Christ in ancient Egypt, China, and India. The insulation value of three layers of fabric was learned early and quilting made its way to England as quilted clothing under the armour of the Crusaders returning from the Middle East. Although quilting and patchwork both existed separately in Europe, it is believed that the marriage of the two into the patchwork quilt happened first in America. European quilts tended to be the more elaborate and expensive applique work. The hardships encountered in the New World, and the scarcity of imported fabric forced women to be resourceful. In their efforts to make ends meet, patches of old clothing were sewn together to make bedcovers. As fabrics became more available, the old idea grew and geometric patchwork quilts blossomed to a new dimension.

Quilting today involves more than just bed covers. Many traditional and contemporary designs are being made on a smaller scale as wallhangings, draperies, tablecloths and clothing. The art, though ancient, has penetrated the modern world and remains a strong statement of beauty in simplicity.

# 2. Amish Quilts From Long Ago

If in defining Amish Quilts one speaks of quilts made by the Amish, they are as abundant today as ever before. Amish women are accomplished artisans in the realm of quiltmaking. Although their style of life and manner of dress is held within strong boundaries, their quilts show great freedom and bright splashes of color.

Amish women today make quilts in a wide variety of patterns. In fact, there is little distinction between those quilts made by Amish and those made by Mennonites or other quilters. Many buy fabrics especially for quilt-making and so carefully coordinate calicoes and solid color fabrics into a well blended whole.

There is another definition of Amish Quilts; those that belong to the era of "what has been." These are the quilts with characteristics making them distinctly different from their contemporaries. The Amish quilts made in the 19th century and up to 1940 had an identity of their own. They were quilts using only the solid colors of Amish clothing in intriguing and unusual ways. The quilting was abundant and exquisite, showing off beautifully in the characteristicly wide solid borders. Quilting thread was often black and the effect on the dark fabrics was a soft sculptured design.

The charm of these earlier quilts is difficult to duplicate. The patterns are often copied but the subtle colors of the natural fibers and the painstaking, expert workmanship are lost to later generations. They stand apart today as a statement of a people with firm roots and strong identity. The colors and patterns are bold and yet there is a restraint and delicate balance maintained with the skilled use of designs held within definite borders. Three of the most commonly recognized Amish patterns are Sunshine and Shadow, Diamond in Square and Bars.

# Sunshine and Shadow

There is something striking, almost shocking about this quilt. Perhaps it is because it is associated with the Old Order Amish whose quiet, subdued manner seems to defy such a statement. Sunshine and Shadow gets its name from the light and dark effect created by the blending and juxtaposition of a large variety of bold solid colors. It is a dramatic quilt but its vibrance is contained inside a strong, solid border.

Sunshine and Shadow is a simple quilt. It is small squares sewn together to form a series of brightly colored expanding squares. Or the squares may be tipped on their sides forming a pattern of concentric diamonds. Its uniqueness is in its use of only solid colors put together in a way that might at first seem odd but on second glance is strangely beautiful.

*Nature continually provides a Sunshine and Shadow motif, as in this photo of an Old Order horse and buggy traveling through a covered bridge.*

*Consisting only of small solid colored squares, the effect of the Sunshine and Shadow quilt is a dramatic juxtaposition of lights and darks. The arrangement of the squares produces a series of expanding diamonds.*

Sunshine and Shadow is an old favorite with Amish quilt-makers. Perhaps the first quilt happened merely by accident—the scraps from the bright solid colors of Amish clothing being used in a functional way. At any rate, its effect was so gripping, so surprising in its boldness that it is a pattern much in demand outside Amish circles even today. Sadly enough, it is almost impossible to recreate the original look. The natural fibers of cotton and wool colored with dyes from nature have a warmth and subtlety not to be achieved in the new synthetics. The colors are blues, maroons, pinks, deep greens, purple, mauves and black—the shades used in Amish shirts and dresses.

The arrangement of the squares is not necessarily Amish. Another quilt, also using small squares in the same arrangement but with printed fabrics would be called Trip Around the World. The Trip Around the World quilt may or may not have a border while the Sunshine and Shadow has a distinctively wide border. It is often elaborately quilted with generous feathers. This quilting represents the work of an experienced artisan. The small continuous curves of the feathers make quilting much more difficult than straight lines or larger patterns.

*Once again the Sunshine and Shadow design, captured here with an Old Order Amish homestead in the winter snow. What may appear cold and apart from the outside is truly warm and vibrant within.*

# Diamond in Square

*Harvest is a time of joy and thanksgiving. Hard work and respect for the earth pay off in the reaping. Here sheaves of wheat mark a Diamond in Square pattern on the field.*

Another Amish quilt using geometric shapes is the Diamond in Square or Center Diamond pattern. This is one large solid color diamond surrounded by a double border—one narrow and one wide. This quilt traditionally uses only three or four colors and they are again colors of Amish clothing—deep, vibrant solids. It is difficult to decide what is more outstanding about this quilt—the bold pattern or the quilting. It is usually quilted in black with the small tight stitches creating a beautiful pattern that softens the sharp lines. Typical quilting pat-

*The exquisite beauty of this quilt is achieved through its generous and fine quilting. The pieces are large and bold and colors are deep vibrant solids. It is an old, old pattern with modern appeal.*

terns would be a circular feather filled with diamonds or a star or tulips. On older quilts grapes and grape leaves may have been used on the narrow border. The Center Diamond quilt is vibrant when its quilting is done masterfully.

# Bars

*Solid colors and bold lines create a statement of strong simplicity. Masterful quilting in abundance gives a soft sculptured effect overall.*

A third example of a traditional Amish design is Bars. Here again the pattern is composed of large pieces of fabric, arranged to form large vertical bars usually in two different solid colors surrounded by a double border. The quilting in the center of the quilt is often less elaborate than in the Center Diamond pattern. Bars may be covered with only small quilted

*A barn forebay reflects the Bars pattern in several ways. Note the door, rafters, and barn window.*

diamonds (cross-hatching) in keeping with the strong straight lines already established. The border however creates a challenge for any avid quilter with an abundance of feathers, cables, or other delicately stitched patterns.

These quilts, although old and traditional, are making a comeback as wallhangings. They appear modern in their boldness both in design and color. The irony of this situation is that the Amish themselves would probably never use them as such.

*Images of roads, paths, and streams occur regularly in nature. These embody the straightforward effect of the Bars quilt.*

# 3. Contemporary Patterns

There is a multitude of quilt patterns and names. Some designs look like what their names imply and other names leave a great deal to the imagination. Many patterns have more than one title. What one quilter calls "Rocky Road to Kansas" another may call "Drunkard's Path." And both are correct. It seems that people created patterns they could identify with but as the situation changed, so did the name. Pattern names may also vary from place to place.

Quilts made by the "plain" groups stand as a statement about peoplehood and creativity. And most everyone responds warmly to this creation and presentation of beauty.

A quilt marries two loves held by the plain people—their love of beauty and their love of work. It is a creation that is at once handsome and functional. That is the real magic of quilting in this setting and the reason for its flourishing among this frugal simple people.

The following patterns are the most commonly found among today's quiltmakers. Some are quite simple; others require great skill.

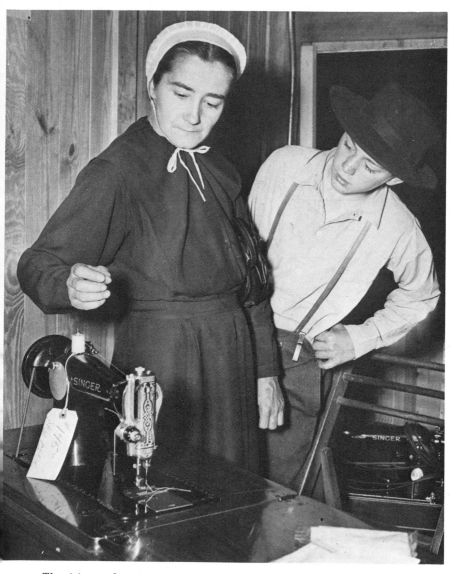

*The rising and setting sun are particularly pronounced in the Amish home. With the absence of electric lights the Amish woman's sewing machine frequently sits directly inside a window where she is surrounded with natural light.*

# Log Cabin

*The Log Cabin is a quilt of infinite variety. Here in a "barnraising" pattern, the light and dark diamond effect is clearly visible. Each patch is a series of "logs" arranged around a center square.*

A barnraising embodies the spirit of community and mutual aid. A quilt is also a statement of unity. Notice the parallels between the quilt and the lines of the emerging barn.

Below: The straight furrow is also translated into a quilt pattern.

The Log Cabin pattern is an old one, probably developed as woman's counterpart to man's building log cabin homes years ago. In its simplicity the design is a delightful example of frugality, warmth and ingenuity.

The Log Cabin quilt became one of the final steps in the recycling of fabrics. Its straight lines and small pieces could utilize almost any fabric scrap that became available. Many a child snuggled in bed under a Log Cabin quilt and looking over the patches could find brother's pajamas, Mom's apron, Dad's old shirt and sister's dress.

There is almost infinite variety in how a Log Cabin quilt can be put together. Occurring most regularly in these quilts is the red center patch. Originally the center square, done in red, symbolized the hearth, the focal point of life in the log cabin. Each patch was then added to the center in much the same way one would stack logs to build a cabin. The Log Cabin pattern remains popular among quiltmakers today but the scrap quilt idea has given way to a well planned and executed color scheme with fabrics purchased specifically for the quilt in mind.

The overall effect of the Log Cabin quilt is determined by the arrangement of light and dark fabrics in the individual patches. The way the patches are put together can create a multitude of designs. An example of this is the Barn Raising. Here lights and darks are arranged around the center patch in an L shape; lights in one corner, darks in the other. The patches are then set in with light and dark sides alternating to the center and then reversing to form a large diamond which repeats itself on the quilt top. This arrangement is also called Trip Around the World.

Another example of the light/dark effect is the design called Courthouse Steps. Here the patches are put together with lights and darks facing each other across the center patch. The patches are assembled with the light sides joining each other, thus forming little clusters of stairways all over the quilt.

Another example is the Straight Furrow. Here again lights and darks are arranged in an L shape around the center square. Each patch is placed opposite the one beside it creating a series of bold diagonal lines across the quilt.

*Other images which remind one of the Log Cabin quilt pattern are pictured above: a row of Old Order Mennonite teams tied at a rail, and the old stairs at the Hans Herr House near Lancaster, Pennsylvania.*

The Log Cabin quilt is relatively easy to put together. All pieces have straight sides and if cut accurately should fit together with very little problem. Quilting on the Log Cabin quilt is usually done following the pattern of the logs. Some quilters prefer quilting along the edge of the patches. This tends to puff and accent each individual log. Others prefer going through the center of the log to avoid having to quilt through any seams. If the quilt has a border there is ample space for more elaborate quilting there.

The Log Cabin quilt remains a favorite among many quilters. When asked why, one woman responded; "They're easy to piece, done in a hurry, and you know how to quilt them."

# Double Wedding Ring

The Double Wedding Ring is an old, old patchwork pattern. It is, as the name implies, two rings interlocked with each other. The effect is striking and varies a great deal depending on the placement of colors forming the rings. Some quilters use their scraps in the Double Wedding Ring because the pieces are quite small. Others plan the quilt with great care alternating light and dark rings. The four "eyes" constituting each ring are connected with four squares angled so as to create four diamonds in each ring.

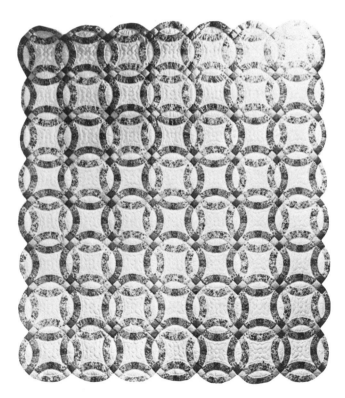

*Circular designs with open spaces provide a pleasing combination of patchwork and quilting expertise. Each ring is a series of small angled patches.*

*Few children experience the fullness of nature as Amish children do. The earth and its creatures are respected as God's creation.*

*Even in the double wheels of the barbed wire roller is an effect similar to the Double Wedding Ring quilt. The detail (right) shows a single patch of that pattern.*

The Double Wedding Ring has a light airy feeling due to the large open spaces inside the rings. The centers are usually done in a light colored fabric to accent the rings and also to show off the quilter's fine stitches. This pattern is done without a border so that the rings create a scalloped edge. Because of the allover pattern the Double Wedding Ring fits nicely on any size bed. Increase or decrease in size is done by dropping or adding another series of rings.

The Double Wedding Ring requires a great deal of skill in piecing because of its circular design. Each ring is made up of tiny angled pieces. Put together, these create a curve to be filled on both sides. The ring is made in four sections. The left "eye" section and top "eye" section are sewn to the center piece. The next group of two "eyes" are put together in the same way and then added to the first until the row is complete. The next step is to begin with the second row starting the same way but the top "eye" of the second row becomes the bottom of the first.

# Dahlia

The Dahlia or Star Flower pattern is yet another variation on a star. This pattern has a unique quality in that it uses gathers to create raised petals surrounding the center of the flower. These puffy petals give the quilt a new dimension and add to its realism. The gathers look very much like the individual petals of the flower by the same name.

This pattern, though more complicated than many patchwork quilts, is not unapproachable. The small gathered petals are the most unusual part and in the words of one quiltmaker, "It's easy except the center. It's a little crooked around there!"

The field of flowers is encompassed by a wide border filled with flowing quilted designs. The finished effect is a pleasing combination of fullness, curves, and clean well defined lines.

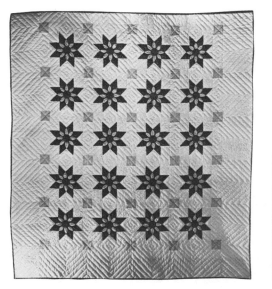

*The Dahlia quilt gets its three dimensional effect from the gathered petals surrounding the center of each flower.*

# Lone Star

*There are numerous quilt patterns dealing with the heavenly bodies. Perhaps this fascination with the sky stems from the fact that so much of rural life begins and ends at the bidding of the sun.*

The Lone Star is one of many patterns dealing with the heavenly bodies. Others are Blazing Star, Sunburst, Broken Star, Feathered Star and numerous other star arrangements. Perhaps this fascination with the sky stems from the fact that so much of rural life begins and ends at the bidding of the sun. The farmer and his wife are awake in time to view the splendor of the sunburst, and perhaps the restful beauty of the first star of evening inspired the Lone Star pattern. The sky is big in the country.

The rising and setting sun are particularly pronounced in the Amish home. With the absence of electric lights the Amish woman's treadle sewing machine frequently sits directly inside

*The Lone Star quilt has the same sense of singleminded purpose, frugal spirit, and unified peacefulness which enriches the Amish world.*

a window where she reaps the full benefit of the natural light. A gas lamp provides ample light for reading or playing checkers at sunset but the coming of darkness surely indicates rest and time for work to cease.

The Lone Star quilt is pieced as a series of diamonds. The small diamonds are pieced in strips and the strips are then connected to form the eight large diamonds that make up the star.

Quilting is generally done following the diamonds in the star but the four empty corners surrounding the star seem always to inspire a burst of imagination and energy in the quilter. This quilting is without a doubt a key part of this quilt's magnificence.

The arrangement of color in a Lone Star is crucial to a feeling of movement outward from the center. There is no mistaking when this arrangement has been accomplished. The quilt seems to burst from the center sending its light dramatically out to the ends of its eight points.

# Fan

The Fan pattern was popular in colonial days when no woman was deemed properly gowned for a social occasion without a fan.

The fan may be done completely by piecework, joining curved seams, or it may be done as a combination of piecing and applique. In the latter case the fan itself is made and then appliqued to a background square. When done in this manner, the edges of the fan are frequently scalloped.

The fan pattern creates different feelings in the way it is put together. The fan patches may be placed each sitting the same way. When arranged in that way it is simple and almost organic in design resembling plants tilting toward the sun. Some quilt historians see an Oriental influence in the repetition of the curved line pattern. The fans may also be placed against each other in a variety of interesting ways, creating colorful circles or rolling lines.

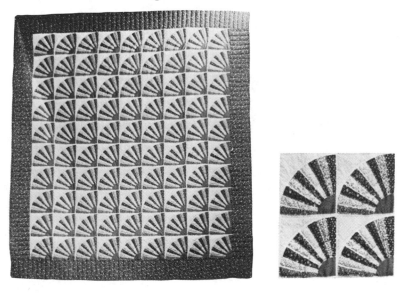

*A simple design, the Fan is almost organic as it resembles plants tilting toward the sun. Variations of the pattern can create colorful circles or falling curves.*

# Tumbling Block

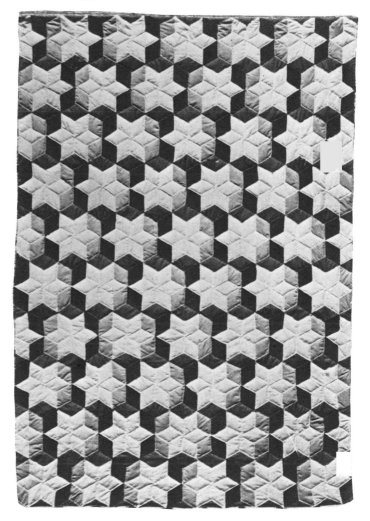

The angles of the diamond shape in this quilt are such that three diamonds form a hexagon. The color combinations can create the optical illusion of stacked cubes. Stars also lie hidden in this design.

The Tumbling Block or Baby Blocks is a simple quilt but its overall effect is filled with intrigue. It is done with only one geometric shape—the diamond. The angles of the diamond are such that three diamonds together form a hexagon. With careful use of light and dark fabrics one can create the optical illusion of stacked cubes.

To achieve this effect, three fabrics of any design may be used—a dark, a medium, and a light colored fabric. The dark is always in one position in the hexagon, the medium in another, and the light in the third. The quilt can also be pieced in a random fashion in which case a star is likely to be the first shape to emerge. It is a pattern that changes as you gaze at it, becoming a series of geometric shapes—diamonds, hexagons, cubes and stars.

The Tumbling Block is pieced either in rows or in small hexagons, added to each other in succession. Quilting is generally done outlining the diamond shapes.

*The picture says it all: fun, togetherness, and tumbling boys.*

*Is it work or fun? A quilting is an all day social affair with a purpose. By the end of*

*p can be completed.*

# Distelfink

*The Pennsylvania Dutch folk art motifs of birds, hearts and flowers are combined here in a gorgeous applique quilt. Expert quilting outlines the applique pieces, giving them a fuller effect.*

Birds and flowers are common Pennsylvania Dutch Folk art motifs. Perhaps the most popular bird is the Distelfink, a charming stylized bird done in bright colors. Although red, yellow, black, and white are the most common, a whole array of colors may be used.

A literal translation of the high German word Distelfink is thistle finch. This name comes from the bird's diet which consists mainly of small, hard, dry seeds found in such plants as the thistle or lettuce. The thistle finch also lines its nest with thistle down. Thus the name thistle finch, salad bird or lettuce bird.

It is thought that the sprightly little bird displayed in the folk art designs is an imaginative combination of both the European and the American finch. The European finch has red in its plumage while the American bird (male species) is yellow and black. The shape of the bird in folk art varies greatly depending on its artist.

Quilters have adapted this design in a variety of ways. It is frequently used along with hearts and tulips in complex applique patches.

*The Distelfink quilt, patterned after the well-known watercolor drawing by nineteenth-century Amish artist Henry Lapp, is shown displayed on a bed built by Lapp.*

# Grandmother's Choice

When asked about this pattern one thoroughly experienced quiltmaker responded: "Anybody can see how to do that." The charm of this pattern is its simplicity. All lines are straight. At first glance one sees the love of geometry that conceives of a patchwork quilt like Grandmother's Choice. But with a longer look at some distance one sees a wild flower pattern—almost feathery in design.

This quilt is frequently done using only two fabrics, one print and one solid (background). The background fabric (usually light in color) is covered with delicate detailed quilting.

The Grandmother's Choice quilt is put together using patchwork in every other block. The alternate block is a square of solid fabric. The finished effect is a series of light-footed X's over the surface of the quilt.

*The magazine and newspaper rack found in many Old Order homes and the protective wire covering the windows of a one-room school remind one of this quilt. Simple and functional.*

Grandmother's Choice is a simple quilt using a combination of geometric shapes. All lines are straight but quilting gives it a soft flowing grace.

# Crazy Quilt

The Crazy Quilt is probably the oldest of quilt patterns. If necessity is indeed the mother of invention, the Crazy Quilt stands as testimony. It speaks of harder times when frugality was a way of life. When cold weather came women turned their energies to providing for their family's warmth. They used the resources available to them. Any scrap or remnant could be used for the Crazy Quilt. Worn-out clothing (cut into pieces) and oddly shaped fabric scraps (generally wool or homespun) were fitted together and stitched with little regard for their similarity in shape, size, or color. The resulting effect was a wonderful hodgepodge of color and a quilt with a story behind each scrap.

These tops were often knotted rather than quilted. Made more for utility than for beauty, these quilts seemed to merit less time in their creation. And they were often made of heavy fabrics with varying consistencies, making quilting extremely laborious. Insulated with wool or cotton, the three layers of a Crazy Quilt certainly took the edge off cold nights.

A later style of Crazy Quilt was worked in blocks. As fabrics became more available women began stitching the scraps to a background block with beautiful, even embroidery stitching often in a contrasting color. Fabrics became more elegant and along with wool and homespun were velvet, brocade, satin,

*There are all shapes and sizes.*

and linen. The blocks were then stitched together to complete the quilt top.

The Crazy Quilt remained prominent for some time for it allowed the use of any available snippet of fabric. Every home had its scrap bag and when its sides bulged a quilt was the likely outcome.

# Friendship Quilt or Album Quilt

There are few gifts of appreciation received more gratefully than a Friendship Quilt.

The Friendship Quilt is a group effort. It is a collection of patches done by different individuals for a mutual friend. The planning of the quilt is done by one person who determines how many patches should be included and how large they should be to make the quilt an adequate size. That person then distributes the patches to other persons who decorate, sign, and return them. The patches are sewn together and a quilting bee is called to complete the quilt.

The occasion to make a Friendship Quilt may be monumental or quite incidental. It is thought that this type of quilt may have been the forerunner of bridal showers. When a girl announced her engagement, her friends would gather, each making a quilt patch and signing her name. There would be a quilting party and the bride-to-be had her first wedding gift.

A Friendship Quilt may also be made by a church sewing circle with different families in the church doing the patches. It would then be presented to a visiting minister at the close of a series of meetings. It may be made by students for a retiring school teacher, family members for a favorite aunt, or anyone deserving of a lasting momento.

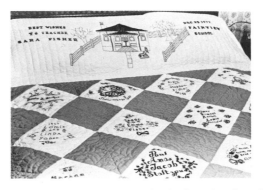

*This Friendship quilt was given to Amish school teacher Sara Fisher by her students in 1977. The quilt on page 57 was given to Mennonite pastor James Hess and his wife Anna by their congregation.*

*The Friendship quilt is a gift of love and respect. The patches are done by different individuals and then quilted. Upon completion, the quilt is presented to a mutual friend.*

# Horn of Plenty

*The Horn of Plenty quilt bespeaks its name with birds and flowers flowing from rich horns. It is an intricate quilt and requires expert workmanship.*

The cornucopia is an ancient symbol of wealth and bounty. Its use in the Horn of Plenty quilt seems quite appropriate. This is an applique quilt with birds and flowers flowing from the horns—a colorful combination of folk design and Oriental influence. Bright solid colors are frequently used giving the quilt a richness and abundant quality.

The quilt is done in a series of nine patches. Five of the nine are saturated with applique work. To give it balance, four interspersed patches are left almost void of applique and are instead occupied by a lovely circular feather quilting design.

This is a sophisticated quilt both in technique and pattern. The applique pieces are small and replete with curves and points. It is work only for an expert quiltmaker. The pattern is showy and exotic. It is without doubt an ornamental quilt.

All this richness is contained within wide quilted borders. In keeping with the fullness of the interior, border designs are generally soft, flowing lines, closely spaced and expertly quilted.

*Gardening and food preservation occupy much of the summer season in an Old Order woman's life. Overflow is frequently sold from roadside stands to eager city dwellers.*

**59**

# Colonial Star

There are two patterns in this quilt—the more forceful stars, and a more subdued pattern of squares and diamonds. The squares are reflected in the deep-set windows of the Hans Herr House on the opposite page. The Herr House is the oldest house in Lancaster County.

The Colonial Star quilt is clean and sharp and as orderly as a Lancaster County garden!

This patchwork quilt is pieced in a series of blocks. First diamond shaped pieces are sewn together to form a star. Then the star points are filled in with squares and triangles making a square block. Finally the blocks are joined with the tips of the stars touching each other. This joining creates another geometric pattern, less forceful than the stars but a common motif in Lancaster County quilts—diamonds and squares. A delicate quilting design fills these open spaces. The stars themselves are quilted around the diamonds giving them a puffy raised quality.

This quilt is frequently planned using only three fabrics—one dark and one light solid alternating for the inner star, a printed fabric for the outer ring, with the dark solid repeated in the farthest point of the star. Placed on a light field, the stars stand out as brilliantly as celestial stars on a clear winter's night.

# Lancaster Rose

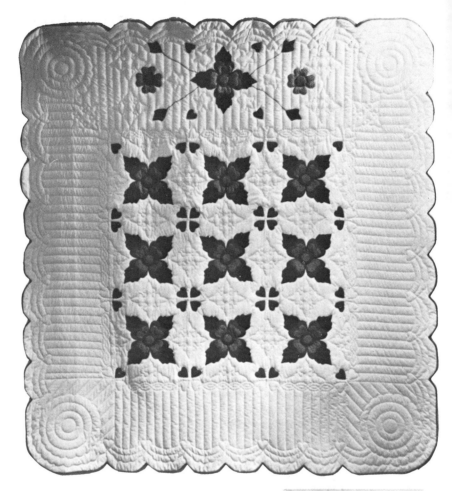

*A simple and clean applique pattern, the Lancaster Rose was created by a Mennonite woman in Lancaster County, Pennsylvania.*

The Lancaster Rose quilt had its beginning in Lancaster County, Pennsylvania. Its creator is an ambitious Mennonite woman who designed it for a class she was to teach. One day when Helen Hess was having a quilting bee some friends from the Pennsylvania Farm Museum at Landis Valley happened by her home. As a result of that visit the Museum asked Helen to teach some quilting classes. Although hesitant she said yes to the offer and plunged in.

In her search for a pattern that was simple and easy, she drove around the County visiting other quilters and asking them for an applique pattern that would be manageable for beginners. She found many avid quiltmakers willing to share their patterns, but few of them were able to articulate instructions about how to do the work. She found that "when people do something well they do it *their* way!" and it is not always easy

*It is little wonder that quiltmakers aspire to capture the grace and beauty of a rose. The Lancaster Rose quilt is one such effort.*

to transmit that information. Eventually she came upon Mrs. Pete Hoover, a Mennonite woman in her upper eighties whom she describes as a "Grandma Moses" in quiltmaking. Mrs. Hoover was working on an Ohio Rose. Thinking it would be a pattern she could use, Helen bought a patch from Mrs. Hoover.

Helen took it home and ripped it apart to examine the pieces. She eliminated, added and redesigned till she arrived at a pattern she both liked and felt comfortable teaching to novice quilters. Her first class worked with the pattern and loved it. Eventually a quilt top of the new design was completed. It was being quilted at the Pennsylvania Farm Museum when a group of women visiting from Ohio asked what the pattern was. They recognized its similarity to the Ohio Rose but knew it was different. Mrs. Hess, who was helping to quilt at the time, wondered aloud why Ohio should be given the credit for such a lovely rose pattern when it already had its own! And so the Lancaster County Rose was born. It was officially christened at a small ceremony in a workshop of the Institute of Pennsylvania Life and Culture in 1970. Its popularity was immediate.

Mrs. Hess does the quilt in a variety of colors. She recommends that the solid color be chosen first, keeping in mind the color scheme of the room in which it will be used. The two prints for the flowers and the leaves should then be coordinated with the solid color. "Nine times out of ten you will have a nice quilt," claims she. The quilt is lovely done in red but certainly should not be restricted to that color.

Historically the rose associated with the city of Lancaster is red. This tradition dates back to a rivalry between the houses of York and Lancaster in England where the red rose symbolized Lancaster and the white rose symbolized York. The names were carried to this side of the ocean where the cities of York and Lancaster are only 30 miles apart.

# Rose of Sharon

This is an old applique pattern probably deriving its name from the Song of Solomon:

> I am the Rose of Sharon
> And the lily of the valleys.
> As the lily among thorns
> So is my love among the daughters;
> As the apple tree among the trees of the wood
> So is my beloved among the sons.

It was considered singularly appropriate for a bride's quilt and was frequently done with pink roses on a white background. These quilts were done with great love and care.

The quilting on a bride's quilt was especially chosen. Hearts were often used (tradition had it that any girl who used hearts in quilting before she had a right to dashed all chances of ever marrying!), surrounded by other delicate designs. It was a quilt for a special occasion and extra time and energies were devoted to it.

Before marriage each girl was to have a full dozen quilts. These would be sufficient to use until her own daughters were old enough to help replenish the supply. The thirteenth quilt, completed after the engagement announcement, was considered the bride's quilt and would adorn the bridal bed.

The Rose of Sharon quilt remains popular today. There is now great diversity in the pattern as well as in colors used.

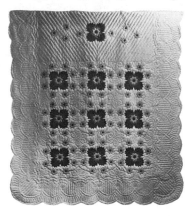

*Beginning as a "bride's quilt," the Rose of Sharon applique pattern has become popular in many variations and colors.*

**65**

# Dresden Plate

The Dresden Plate is a combination of piecing and applique. The petals of the plate are pieced together, then the whole circle is appliqued to the background patch.

The Dresden Plate quilt name is based on a popular china made in Dresden, Germany between the early 1700's and the late 1800's. This delicate porcelain was decorated in a variety of bright colors and gold.

The pattern is a combination of both patchwork and applique. The petal-shaped wedges of the plate are pieced together and the complete plate and the center circle are appliqued to a square patch. In its original form, each of the petals in the plate had a curved outer edge. As it passed from one quiltmaker to another it underwent changes so that frequently it is seen with pointed rather than rounded edges. Both varieties are lovely; the points are more easily appliqued than the curves.

The Dresden Plate can be a delightful scrap quilt or a lovely color coordinated quilt. The center circle is usually done in a solid color fabric which may or may not also appear in the wedges.

*Buggy wheels in this scene from Sugar Creek, Ohio, remind one of the Dresden Plate quilt.*

# Grandmother's Flower Garden

Nature has inspired many quilt patterns but few are as realistically carried out as in the Grandmother's Flower Garden or Honeycomb. This pattern uses hexagons, a very old form of geometric patchwork. Historically, hexagons have appeared in hundreds of mosaic designs on buildings and floors. Arrangement can be random or the hexagons may be arranged to form rosettes, diamonds, triangles, stars, etc. In a random arrangement the quilt top very much resembles a honeycomb. One can almost taste the sweetness buried in the soft richness of the quilt.

A more studied arrangement is the Grandmother's Flower Garden. Here the quilt is put together by making a series of small flowers or rosettes. One hexagon forms the center. Six more of another color surround that and then twelve more are added to form a brightly colored flower. These are then set together with a row of green as foliage or with another color to form a path through the quilt. Thus one creates a garden that

*Flowers adorn this world. The splash of nature is cultivated while austerity is encouraged in the fashion of one's clothes.*

*Hexagons are the basis of this quilt pattern. They may be set randomly or they may be carefully arranged to form little rosettes as in the quilt above.*

invites visitation and admiration of each individual flower.

This is no task for a novice quiltmaker. Matching six points on one little two inch patch is not easy. However, with the proper care this one can go together with relative ease. The Honeycomb or random arrangement can be pieced in strips and then sewed row upon row. The Flower Garden is pieced by making the individual flowers and then adding the path.

*Grandmas love to create new quilts. Grandpas sometimes take down old ones. The bonnets enjoy the sun.*

# President's Wreath

Wreaths of many varieties have always seemed to delight quilters. There is the Bridal Wreath, the Rose Wreath, Wreath of Flowers, President's Wreath, and others.

The President's Wreath became popular in the late 1800's. It was given its name during the Civil War and was associated with President Lincoln. It has maintained that name through the years. It is a handsome and dignified quilt that seems to justify its regal title.

It is an applique quilt with enough open space to give the quilter ample room to demonstrate quilting ability along with a skilled appliqueing technique.

*Wreaths of many varieties have always seemed to delight quiltmakers. The Presidents Wreath is a dignified applique quilt that has been associated with President Lincoln.*

# Wandering Foot or Turkey Tracks

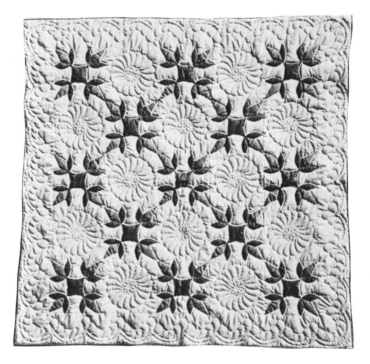

Turkey Tracks is an old pattern seldom seen or used today. One obvious reason is its difficulty. The pieces are small and curved, both of which discourage many people at the onset. Another reason for its scarcity may be an old superstition associated with the pattern. Tradition has it that any boy who slept under such a quilt would eventually leave home and begin a life of aimless wandering. No mother wanted to take that risk. The easiest way to avoid the possibility was to change the quilt name. And so Wandering Foot became Turkey Tracks and who could fear that?

Wandering Foot can be a lovely scrap quilt with each patch being different. Somehow this seems to be true to its name. However, it can be just as striking with each identical patch firmly placed and enclosed in a quilted border.

*The popular belief that the young people leave the Plain communities is false.*
*Some have a wandering foot, but more than three-fourths choose to stay.*

# Drunkard's Path

This is a pattern that changes its name as well as its appearance depending on the way it is put together. The Drunkard's Path consists of a square with a crescent shape cut out of its one corner. It is pieced using a light and dark fabric, the fabrics being interchanged in the blocks. The finished effect is tantalizing. In the Drunkard's Path variation, the visual image is quite clear. It is a twisted, rambling trail, difficult to maneuver. This same arrangement is also called Rocky Road to Dublin or Rocky Road to California, or Robbing Peter to Pay Paul. Other variations on the same pattern are Love Ring or Nonesuch, Fool's Puzzle and Wonder of the World.

The Drunkard's Path pattern requires some skill in piecing because of its curves. It also requires a clear mind to assemble it, making sure to bring all the right corners together!

*It's easy to guess how this quilt with its rambling curves got its variety of names.*

# Old Country Tulip

Designing your own quilt patch is really not difficult. All you need is some inspiration and enthusiasm. I got the inspiration one day and shared it with artist Beth Oberholtzer who added an abundance of enthusiasm. Together we worked out something we felt was representative of our home area (Lancaster County)—relatively simple to do, and aesthetically pleasing. Tulips and hearts seemed right together and Beth came up with a sharp, clean "Old Country Tulip" design. We tried a sample patch and agreed that it was presentable. The first quilt was done in a variety of colors, each patch being different. It is displayed in The Old Country Store in Intercourse, Pennsylvania, for which it was named.

*The first Old Country Tulip quilt was completed at a quilting held at the home of veteran quilter Emma Weaver (second from left.) Author Rachel Pellman is seated far left.*

# 4. How to Make a Quilt

Quilts, as we know them today, have three layers: the decorative top, the lining or batting and a back.

The decorative quilt top is usually pieced or appliqued. To make a pieced top, small pieces of fabric are simply stitched together to form a design. For an appliqued top, pieces are cut from whole fabric, then applied onto a large background of fabric to create the design.

*To make a pieced top, pattern pieces must be accurately marked and cut. They are then sewn together, making sure all corners and points fit precisely.*

*Children often accompany their mothers to a quilting bee. The stretched frame makes a wonderful playhouse. Children may also be asked to keep a supply of threaded needles on hand.*

For applique work the design pieces are cut from fabric with a ¼ inch seam allowance on all sides. (Many quilters prefer to mark the pieces in actual size without the seam allowance and then cut ¼ inch around the marking line.) This ¼ inch allowance is then folded under (to the marked line) and basted in place. Basting the seam allowances under before appliqueing the pieces allows greater accuracy in keeping their curves rounded and their points sharp. The basted piece is then appliqued to the background fabric.

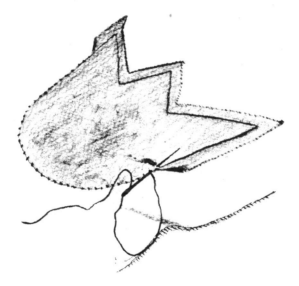

*Applique work requires expert craftsmanship. Stitches must be small, tight, and nearly invisible.*

The applique stitch is tiny and tight, hidden away in the basted fold of the appliqued piece and on the underside of the background fabric. It is best to use thread that matches the color of the piece being appliqued.

Reverse applique happens when instead of appliqueing a piece of fabric onto another background piece, two layers of fabric are put together, a design is snipped out of the top piece and a tiny hem is folded under creating a window effect for the design. The same stitch is used.

Applique work may be done on a series of blocks or patches that are then stitched together to make the quilt top. Or it may be done on a single piece of fabric large enough to cover the surface of the bed.

Some quilts are neither pieced nor appliqued. Instead their tops and backs are a solid color fabric which is quilted in elaborate designs. Without prints or piecing to detract, the stitching takes center stage in these quilts.

The batting or lining of a quilt today is usually a synthetic fiberfill. It is lightweight, washable and retains its puffy quality. It has subsequently largely replaced cotton or wool batting.

The third layer of the quilt is the backing. It is fabric of similar weight to that of the top. The backing may repeat a fabric used on the top of the quilt or it may be entirely different. Some people prefer the versatility of a contrasting fabric. Others select a solid color fabric that shows off the quilting.

*A quilt consists of three layers: top, batting and back. These are held together with quilting which goes through all the layers (see inset.)*

The top, batting, and backing are joined by short running stitches called quilting, which gives its name to the whole. The quilting stitches follow a decorative pattern marked on the quilt top.

An alternate method of joining the three layers is to knot them together. Knotting is used primarily in comforters which are usually less decorative since they are made primarily for warmth. Comforters are often made of a heavy weight fabric and thick batting, making quilting difficult. So at regular intervals across the top, heavy thread is drawn through the thick layers, knotted, and then clipped off.

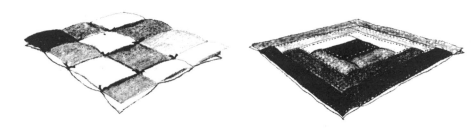

*A comforter, used primarily for warmth, is usually less decorative. It is therefore knotted (left) rather than quilted (right) to hold the three layers together.*

## Where to Begin?

Quilts make very personal statements about their makers. As they pass from generation to generation they become treasured records of family history.

Quiltmakers create statements about themselves, told by the pattern they choose, the colors they blend and their workmanship.

So careful thought should be part of a quilt's production. There are preliminary questions: How will the quilt be used? If it is the highlight of an already furnished bedroom, color and pattern need to be carefully coordinated with other furnishings. A parent or grandparent making a quilt for the next generation may choose a pattern which best accentuates the color they want to use. In any case, fabric choice is best done in an orderly manner, rather than on impulse.

# Choosing a Quilt Pattern

Making a quilt for a particular room that is already furnished, means taking into account the size of the room and how full it is. The quilt should blend well and not overpower its surroundings. If on the other hand, the room is to be planned around the quilt, the bed covering may be a bolder statement of color and pattern.

One's pattern choice has a bearing on color options, as well. The quiltmaker must determine how many colors of fabric the pattern calls for, and, for best effect, whether the colors should be highly contrasting, with dark and light shades or be a subtle blending of color. Secondary colors, planned well, enliven a pattern, also.

# Determining Size

The size of the bed for which a quilt is being made should also be considered when choosing the quilt's pattern. If the design has a large central medallion or star, most of it should fit on top of the mattress. Or if the quilt is made up of blocks, enough blocks should fit on top of the mattress so that the pattern is effective.

Quilts are primarily decorative bed covers. They are not usually made to reach to the floor as a bedspread does. A quilt should be wide enough to cover the mattress and it sides. Some cover the box spring as well. (Frequently commercially made dust ruffles are used to fall below the quilt to the floor.)

Before setting the quilt's size, it is important to measure the mattress, adding width to cover the sides of the mattress and boxspring. If the quilt is to cover the pillows, length should be allowed for that, as well as a few extra inches for tucking under the pillows. The quilt should hang over the end of the bed about the same amount as it does at the sides.

It is helpful to sketch the proposed quilt to scale on graph paper and then color it to get a sense of the overall finished design before beginning the project. Such an exercise will show whether the pattern fits the bed and whether the length allowed to tuck under the pillow will disrupt the overall pattern.

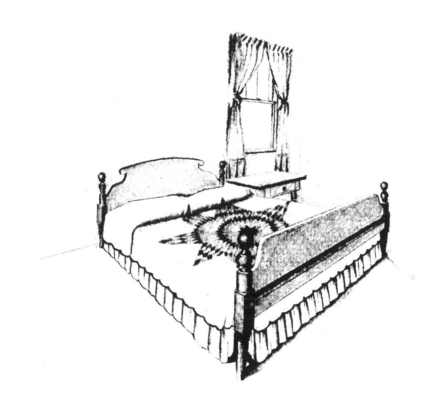

*If the quilt design has a large central medallion or star, most of it should fit on top of the mattress. Borders should be wide enough to allow for an adequate pillow tuck as well as enough overhang on sides and end to meet the dust ruffle.*

# Figuring Fabric Requirements

Many quilt patterns list fabric requirements. But there may be items that are not spoken to. Quilts are usually bound by matching fabric cut on the bias. Sometimes extra yardage is allowed for on the back which can be turned over and hemmed on the front. In either case, length for binding should be considered when purchasing quilt fabric.

Old patterns often without instructions, may not include seam allowances on pattern pieces. Additional yardage is needed for that. The pattern may call for long borders of fabric or long strips of sash between pattern blocks. One should have sufficient fabric so that borders need not be pieced. Throughout the quilt all pieces should be cut with the grain of the fabric.

# Choosing Fabrics

For the best effect, the same type and weight of fabric should be used throughout a quilt. Cottons are durable and wear well. A dacron and polyester blend may be used with good results.

A very dark fabric chosen for the back of the quilt may shine through and mar the effect of the front of the quilt.

Some quiltmakers use sheets for backing since that eliminates any seams in the back of the quilt. However, sheets may be more difficult to quilt because of their tight weave.

It is wise when selecting quilt fabric to buy a bit more than needed. Too often quiltmakers have gone back for more, only to find it no longer available.

All fabric should be washed to pre-shrink it before use.

# Cutting Fabric

One should never assume that a pattern passed through family generations or published in a reliable magazine is absolutely right. It is best to cut and sew one complete patch as a test before cutting the entire quilt.

Pattern pieces (templates) can be made of a variety of materials. Old family patterns are often made of cardboard. Cardboard works well as long as the edges do not get worn down and thereby affect the measurement of the pattern. Veteran quiltmakers glue a piece of fine sandpaper to their cardboard pattern to help hold it in place as they mark the fabric. Today, templates are also made from durable plastic or metal.

If the ¼ inch seam allowance has not been added to the pattern, it should be as the fabric is being marked. Fabric may be marked with pencil; light-colored lead used on darker fabric; darker lead on lighter fabric. Marking and cutting should be done with the grain of the fabric to prevent pieces from stretching out of shape as they are sewn together.

# Assembling

There are a variety of opinions about assembling a quilt. Some insist that all sewing must be done by hand. Others opt for the sewing machine. Whichever method is used, it is essential that seam lines be followed so that pieces meet exactly where they are supposed to. This is meticulous work. But anything less will result in disappointment to the quiltmaker when the quilt is finished.

When all the pieces are finally cut, the best place to work at assembling them may be the floor. Finally one gets to see the overall effect of the quilt.

# Marking the Quilting Design

The quilting design adds a completely new dimension to the pieced or appliqued quilt top. It softens the straight lines of borders and sashes and gives large expanses of unpieced areas, a beauty of their own.

Quilting designs can be drawn on light colored fabric with a soft lead pencil. On darker fabric, dressmaker's chalk can be used and later easily brushed off. Quilting lines should be marked as lightly as possible. Few people want to wash their quilt when it is brand new and if marking is done discretely there will be no reason to. It is wise to test the marking utensil on sample fabric first to make sure there will be no unsightly lines on the finished quilt.

On light colored fabrics, quilting designs can be placed under the fabric and simply traced. On darker fabric, cardboard patterns can be traced around with light colored dressmakers' chalk. On many patchwork or pieced quilts much of the quilting follows stitch lines and need not be marked.

*There is no denying the fact that life in the Old Order Amish and Mennonite communities is dramatically disciplined. But these boundaries have distinct advantages. There is freedom in knowing limits and inside these limits is great room to grow.*

## "Putting In"

The traditional quilting frame accommodates between ten and twelve women. It is a simple structure: four long bars of wood clamped together at corners and set on wooden sawhorses, chairs or specially made wooden posts. On each of the four lengths of wood heavy cotton fabric is tacked. The quilt backing is stretched and pinned to the fabric-lined boards. The batting is laid on next and

**85**

finally the quilt top is stretched across and also pinned. Quilting starts along all four edges and progresses to the center by means of rolling the finished quilt onto the two end rails and re-clamping those rails to the stationary side rails.

When no one is working on it, the quilt is covered with a large sheet to keep it clean. Such a quilt frame also makes a wonderful playhouse for children!

Quilting has come to suburbia and the city but the traditional quilting frame does not fit into most homes today. Quilting frames have been adapted to smaller spaces and to the individual quilter. A popular frame today is one which accommodates the full width of a quilt, but on which the length is rolled from rail to rail, set about 18 inches apart.

There are also a variety of lap hoops and frames that are much more portable and can accommodate large and small projects alike. When using a lap hoop or frame the three layers of the quilt need to be carefully pinned together before quilting begins.

# Quilt Care

A quilt is a handcrafted work of art. To preserve its life and beauty it must be well cared for. Antique quilts are in a category of their own. One should seek professional help before attempting to clean, repair or store old quilts. Their fibers weaken with age and exposure so they must be handled delicately.

New quilts are usually made of 100% cotton or cotton/ polyester blended fabrics which are machine washable. The batting used today is often polyester which is also washable. However, when a large mass of fabric three layers thick is held together simply with quilting stitches, it is advisable to put as little tension as possible on those threads. Therefore, if the quilt is washed, it should be done gently and with cool water. (Very deep colored fabrics may bleed in water so that dry cleaning may be preferable.)

Drying in a drying machine on a low setting should be

*Quilts seem to embody the spirit of peoplehood. There is a sense of unity, strength, and vibrance in the balancing and blending of many parts and colors.*

safe. The quilt may be hung outdoors to dry but should be draped over several clotheslines to distribute its weight more evenly. Or it may be laid flat on the grass over absorbent towels.

A quilt is made to be enjoyed and used. However, when storing a quilt, it should be rolled rather than folded to prevent permanent creases. (Rolling over a cardboard tube works well.) If storage space necessitates folding it should be taken out periodically and refolded so that lasting lines are not created.

When stored, a quilt should be wrapped in a sheet, pillowcase or something that allows it to breathe. It should never be kept in plastic. One should also be alert that it is protected from insect damage.

# Glossary

**AMISH**—The name identifying one of the most conservative Anabaptist groups established in 1693. A Christian group, these people live lives of firm discipline apart from the larger society but support and maintain their beliefs within a strong sense of community.

**ANABAPTIST**—The nickname meaning "rebaptizer," given to the radical group who advocated adult baptism during the Protestant reformation. They believed the church should be a group of adults, voluntarily baptised upon confession of faith.

**APPLIQUE**—The process of applying one piece of fabric to the surface of another. The pieces are usually cut in decorative shapes and then sewn to the surface of another piece of fabric with tiny hidden stitches.

**BACKING**—The underside of a quilt.

**BARNRAISING**—The practice of rebuilding with volunteer labor a barn that has been destroyed. Amish, Mennonite and other community men gather for a day of work and socializing to build the bulk of the structure.

**BATTING**—The middle layer of a quilt which provides its insulation value. The puffy quality of the batting also accentuates the quilting designs, giving it a three dimensional effect. Batting today is usually 100% polyester.

**BINDING**—The final step in quiltmaking. Binding finishes off by turning under or turning inside the raw edges around the four sides of the quilt.

**BORDER**—The fabric frame around the edge of a patchwork or applique quilt top.

**CROSS-HATCHING**—The name given to the quilting design of diagonal lines criss-crossing the surface of a quilt. The overall effect is a series of small diamonds.

**DISTELFINK**—A small bird commonly used in Pennsylvania Dutch folk art designs.

**FEATHERS**—The name given to a delicately curved, plumed quilting design.

**HEXAGON**—A geometric form with six sides frequently used in quiltmaking.

**KNOTTING**—An alternative to quilting. Knotting is done primarily in comforters which are less decorative since they are used primarily for warmth. Heavy thread is drawn through the three layers, knotted, and then clipped off.

**MARKING**—The process of drawing the design onto the quilt

top for quilting. Marking also applies to the tracing of pattern pieces before cutting.

**MENNONITE**—An Anabaptist group formed in the early 16th century. Usually less outwardly conservative than the Amish, this group too believes in separation from the world and radical discipleship to Jesus Christ.

**MENNONITE CENTRAL COMMITTEE**—The inter-Mennonite relief organization that supplies food, clothing, community development workers, and financial aid overseas and throughout North America.

**OLD ORDER**—A descriptive term used by the authors to designate those among the Mennonites and Amish who take their cues for decision-making primarily from their faith fellowship instead of the larger world.

**PATCH**—A small piece of fabric joined with other small pieces to form a quilt top. The joining of these patches is called piecing.

**PUTTING-IN**—The process of stretching the three layers of a quilt into a quilt frame for quilting.

**QUILT**—A decorative bed cover consisting of a top, batting and backing. The three layers are held together with quilting, a series of tiny, tight stitches done in a decorative pattern and connecting all three layers. To quilt is the process of applying the stitches. This may be done by an individual or at a quilting bee or quilting, where several women gather to work together on a quilt.

**QUILT FRAME**—The mechanism used to keep the three layers of the quilt tautly stretched together for quilting. There are many varieties of quilt frames ranging from hoops which accomodate only one patch to a large floor model frame which exposes the full surface of the quilt.

**QUILT TOP**—The most decorative layer of the quilt which is usually done in either patchwork or applique.

**TEMPLATES**—Pattern pieces for quilt patches or quilting designs. These may be made of cardboard, plastic, metal or other durable materials.

# Readings and Sources

Bacon, Lenice Ingram. **American Patchwork Quilts.** William Morrow and Company, Inc., New York, New York, 1973.

**Berks Historical Review.** Volume 11, pp. 102–106.

——————. Volume 20, pp. 121–128.

Beyer, Jinny. **Patchwork Patterns.** EPM Publications, McLean, Virginia, 1979.

Bishop, Robert and Safanda, Elizabeth. **A Gallery of Amish Quilts.** E. P. Dutton and Company, Inc., New York, New York, 1976.

Carlisle, Lilian Baker. **Pieced Work and Applique Quilts at Shelburne Museum.** The Shelburne Museum, Shelburne, Vermont, 1957.

Colby, Averil. **Quilting.** Charles Scribner's Sons, New York, New York, 1971.

Cooper, Patricia and Buferd, Norma Bradley. **The Quilters: Women and Domestic Art.** Anchor Press/Doubleday, Garden City, New York, 1978.

Frager, Dorothy. **The Quilting Primer.** Chilton Book Company, Radnor, Pennsylvania, 1974.

Good, Merle and Good, Phyllis Pellman. **20 Most Asked Questions about the Amish and the Mennonites.** Good Books, Lancaster, Pennsylvania, 1979.

Gutcheon, Beth. "Quilting: Step by Step Instructions for Making a Patchwork Quilt," **Country Journal,** March 1981, pp. 38–48.

Haders, Phyllis. **Sunshine and Shadow: The Amish and Their Quilts.** Universe Books, New York, New York, 1976.

Hall, Carrie A. and Kretsinger, Rose G. **The Romance of the Patchwork Quilt in America.** Bonanza Books, New York, New York, 1935.

Hassel, Carla J. **You Can Be A Super Quilter!** Wallace-Homestead Book Company, Des Moines, Iowa, 1980.

Hinson, Delores A. **Quilting Manual.** Dover Publications, Inc., New York, New York, 1970.

Holstein, Jonathan. **The Pieced Quilt: An American Design Tradition.** New York Graphic Society, Boston, Massachusetts, 1973.

Hostetler, John A. **Amish Society.** Johns Hopkins University Press, Baltimore, Maryland, 1980.

Houck, Carter and Miller, Myron. **American Quilts and How To Make Them.** Charles Scribner's Sons, New York, New York, 1975.

Ickis, Marguerite. **The Standard Book of Quiltmaking and Collecting.** Dover Publications, Inc., New York, New York, 1949.

Khin, Yvonne M. **The Collector's Dictionary of Quilt Names and Patterns.** Acropolis Books, Ltd., Washington, D.C., 1980.

King, Elizabeth. **Quilting.** Leisure League of America, New York, New York, 1934.

Leman, Bonnie. **Quick and Easy Quilting.** Moon Over the Mountain Publishing Company, Denver, Colorado, 1972.

Leman, Bonnie. **Log Cabin Quilts.** Moon Over the Mountain Publishing Company, Denver, Colorado, 1980.

Lichten, Frances. **Folk Art Motifs of Pennsylvania.** Hastings House Publishers, New York, New York, 1954.

Mahler, Celine Blanchard. **Once Upon a Quilt: Patchwork Design and Technique.** Van Nostrand Reinhold Company, New York, New York, 1973.

Malone, Maggie. **Classic American Patchwork Quilt Patterns.** Sterling Publishing Company, New York, New York, 1980.

McKim, Ruby. **101 Patchwork Patterns.** Dover Publications, Inc., New York, New York, 1962.

Murwin, Susan Aylsworth and Payne, Suzzy Chalfant. **Quick and Easy Patchwork on the Sewing Machine.** Dover Publications, Inc., New York, New York, 1979.

**Pennsylvania Dutchman.** Volume 1, No. 24, p. 1.

——————————. Volume 5, No. 10, p. 16.

**Pennsylvania Folklife.** Volume 13, No. 3, p. 2.

——————————. Volume 21, Supplement, p. 31.

Peto, Florence. **American Quilts and Coverlets.** Chanticleer Press, New York, New York, 1949.

Puckett, Marjorie and Giberson, Gail. **Primarily Patchwork.** Cabin Craft, Redlands, California, 1975.

Robertson, Elizabeth Wells. **American Quilts.** The Studio Publications, Inc., New York, New York, 1948.

Schiffer, Margaret B. **Historical Needlework of Pennsylvania.** Charles Scribner's Sons, New York, New York, 1968.

# Index

Joanne Ranck                    Rachel T. Pellman

Rachel (Thomas) Pellman is a Lancaster County native, the youngest in a family of 3 sisters and 6 brothers. She is presently manager of The Old Country Store in Intercourse, PA. The store specializes in quilts, fabrics, and other quality hand-crafted items. A seamstress and quilter herself, Rachel appreciates the painstaking effort and care involved in quilt-making. Much of the information for the booklet was gleaned from the stories and examples of numerous quilters who make frequent visits to The Old Country Store.

Rachel is a graduate of Eastern Mennonite College with a degree in Home Economics Education. She and her husband Kenny live in Lancaster and attend Rossmere Mennonite Church. Rachel is known to many as Hazel for her role in the motion picture **HAZEL'S PEOPLE.**

Joanne Ranck also grew up in Lancaster County. She graduated from Eastern Mennonite College with a degree in English. She and her husband, Douglas Dirks, are presently living in Victoria, British Columbia. They plan a term of overseas service under Mennonite Central Committee in the immediate future.

Joanne worked for four years as manager of The People's Place in Intercourse, PA. where she launched the sales of high quality quilts. Joanne enjoys sewing and quilting. Her friends and family have been grateful recipients of many handmade gifts.